Afghc

Trace Taylor

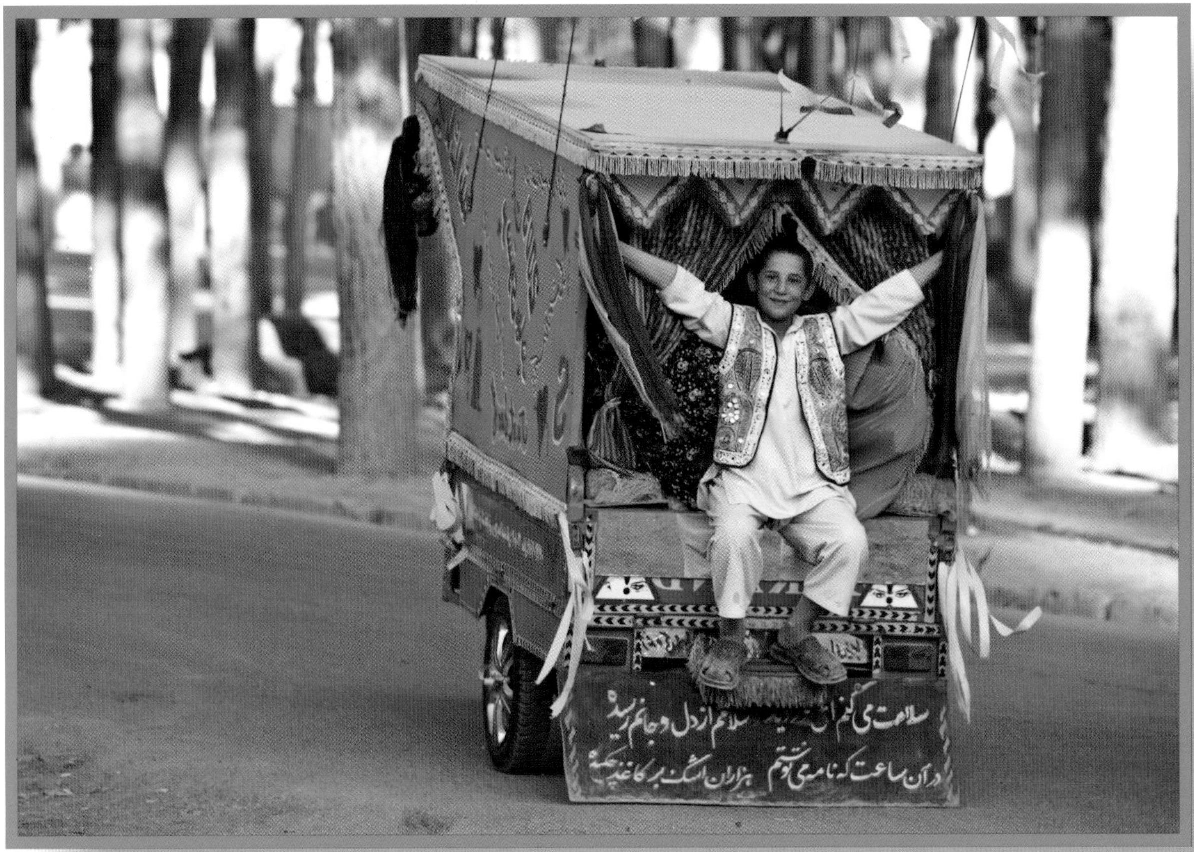

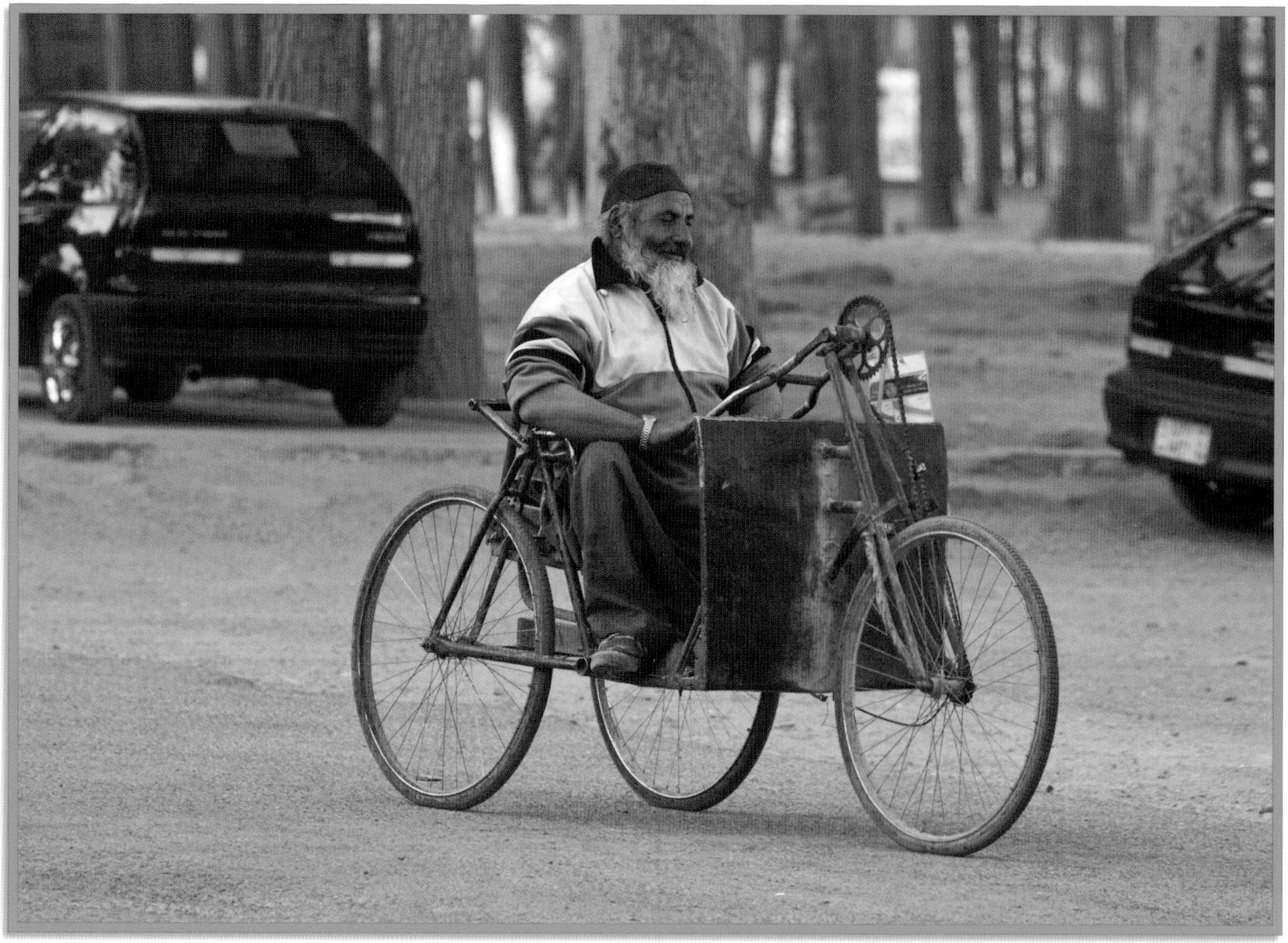

bicycle

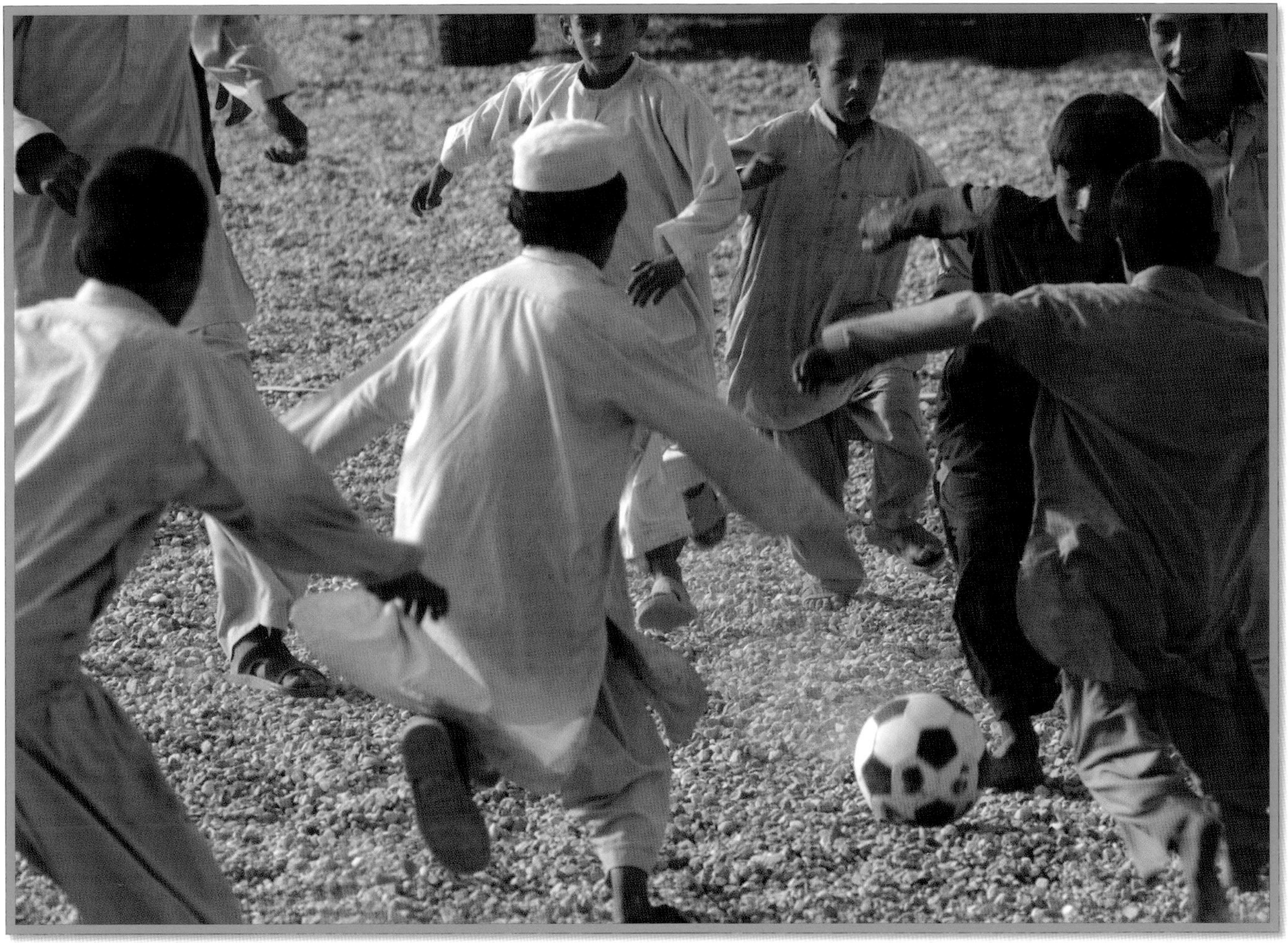

ball

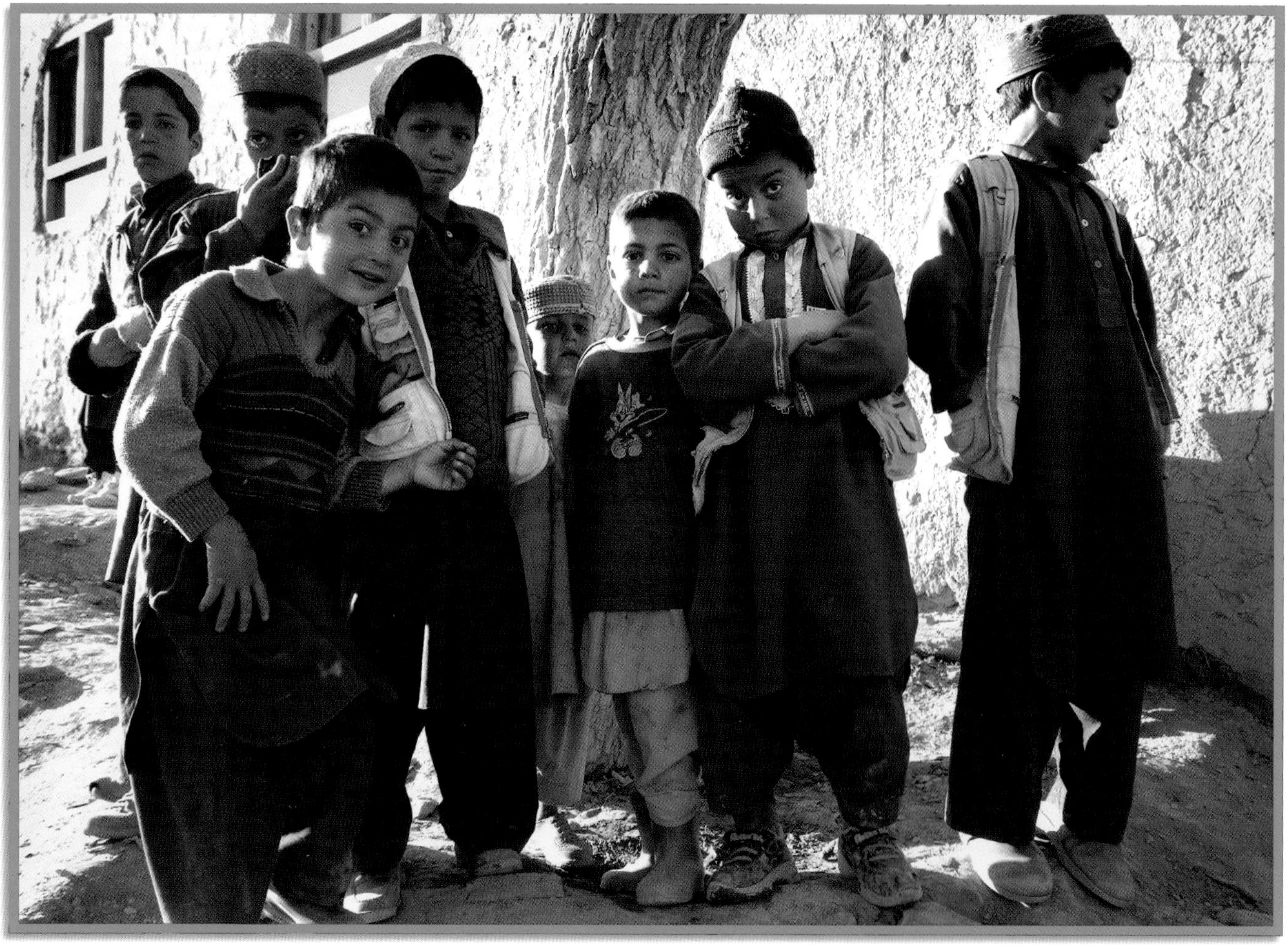

boys

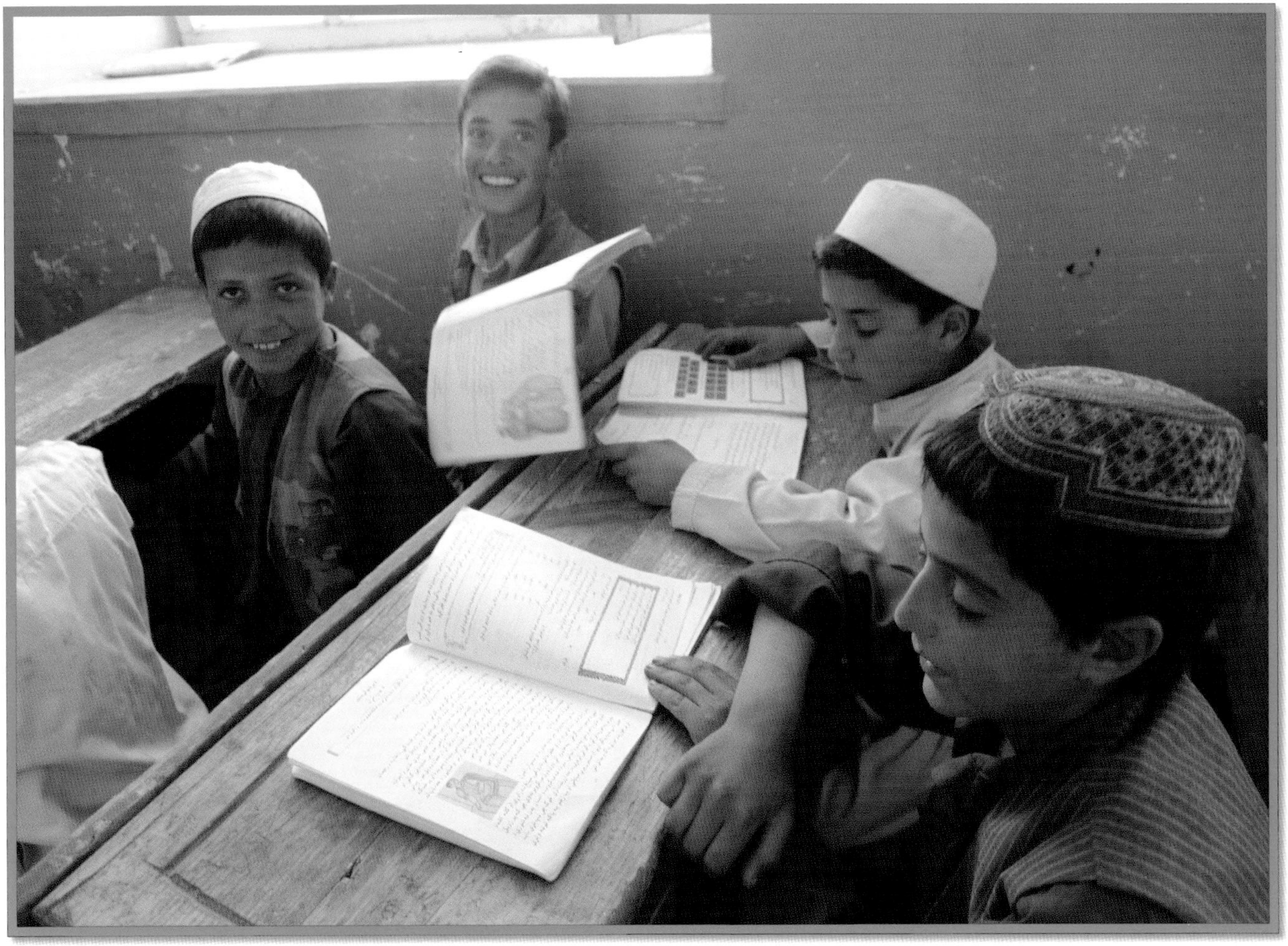

books

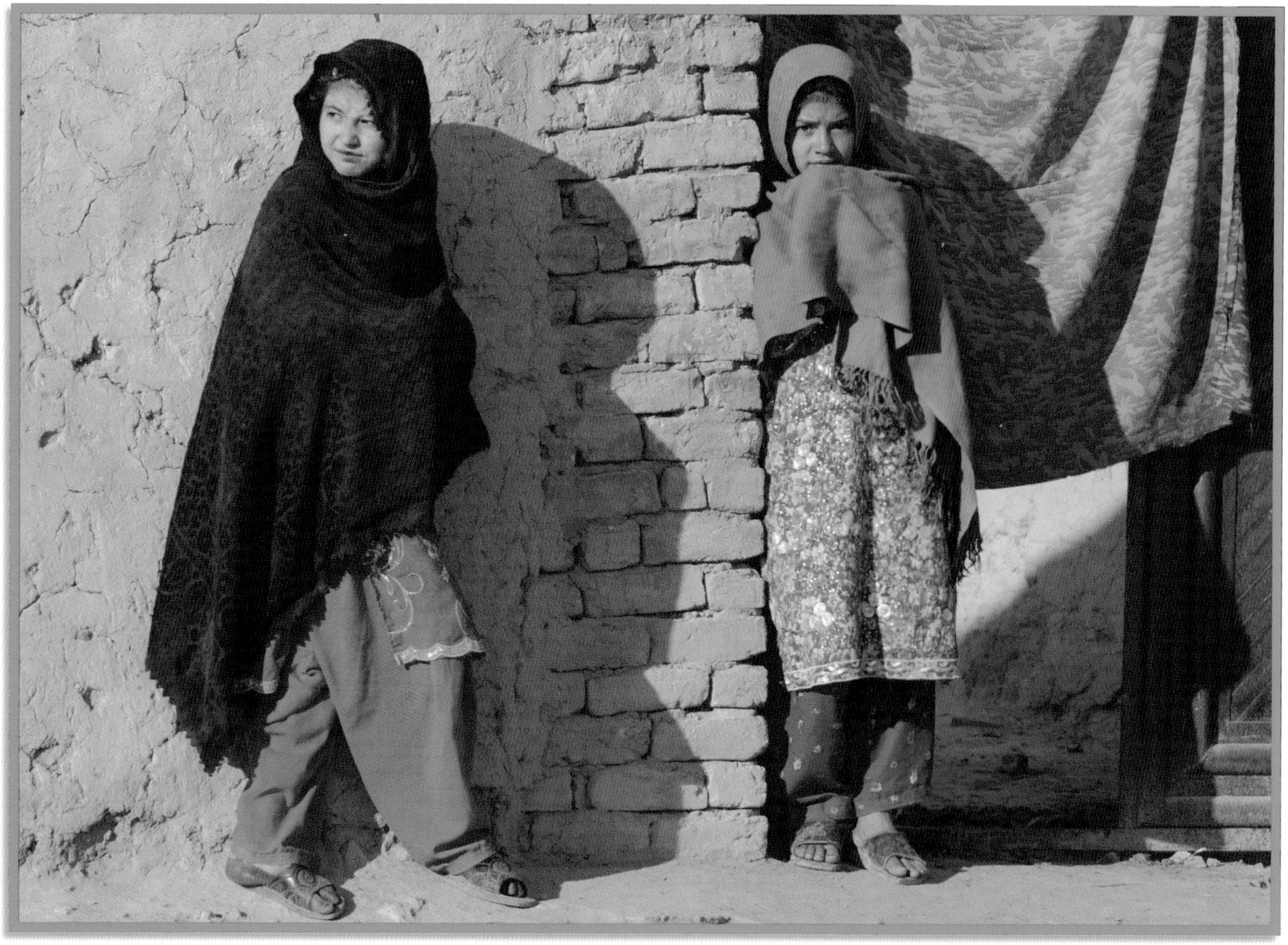

girls

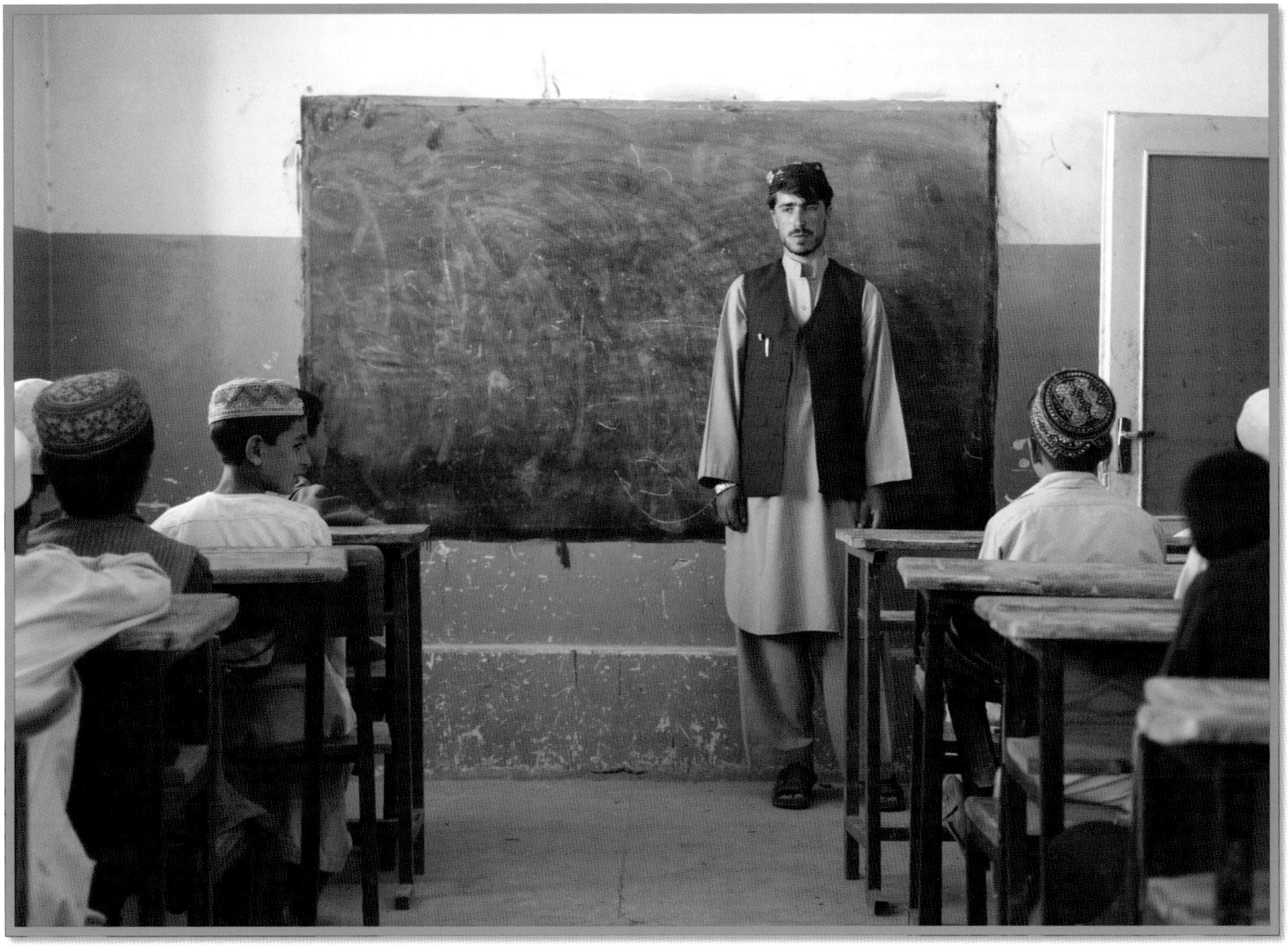

school

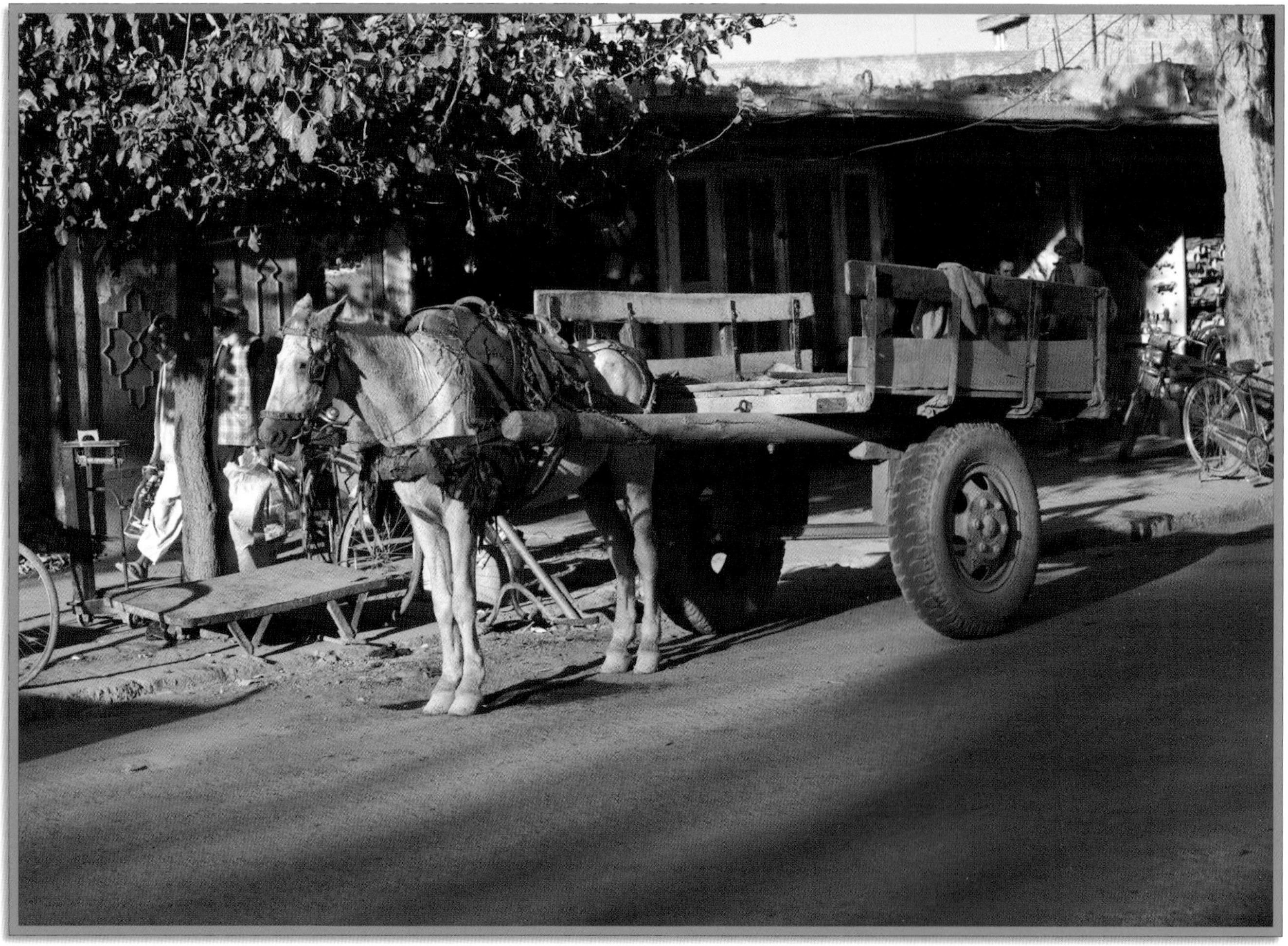

horse

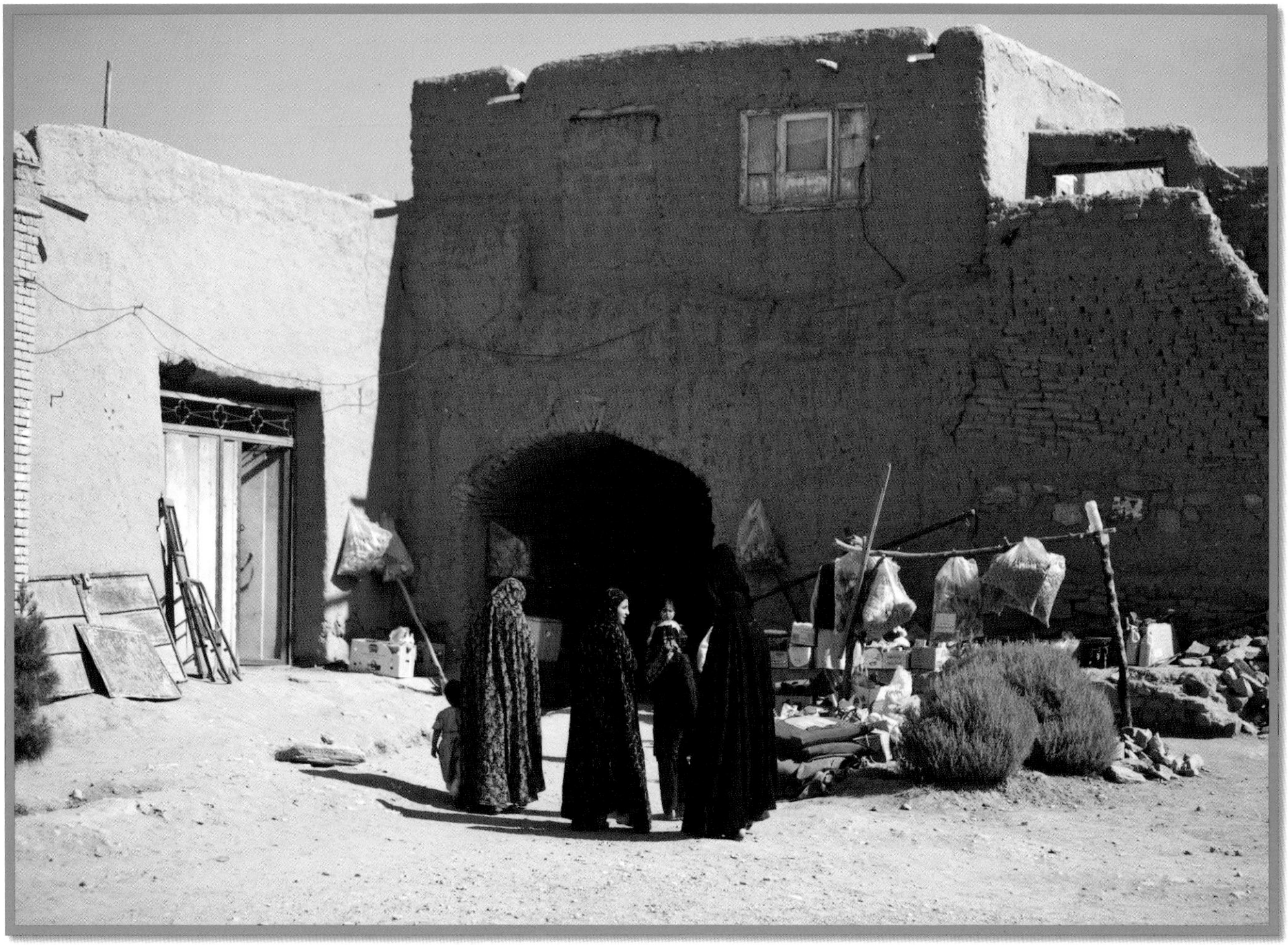

house

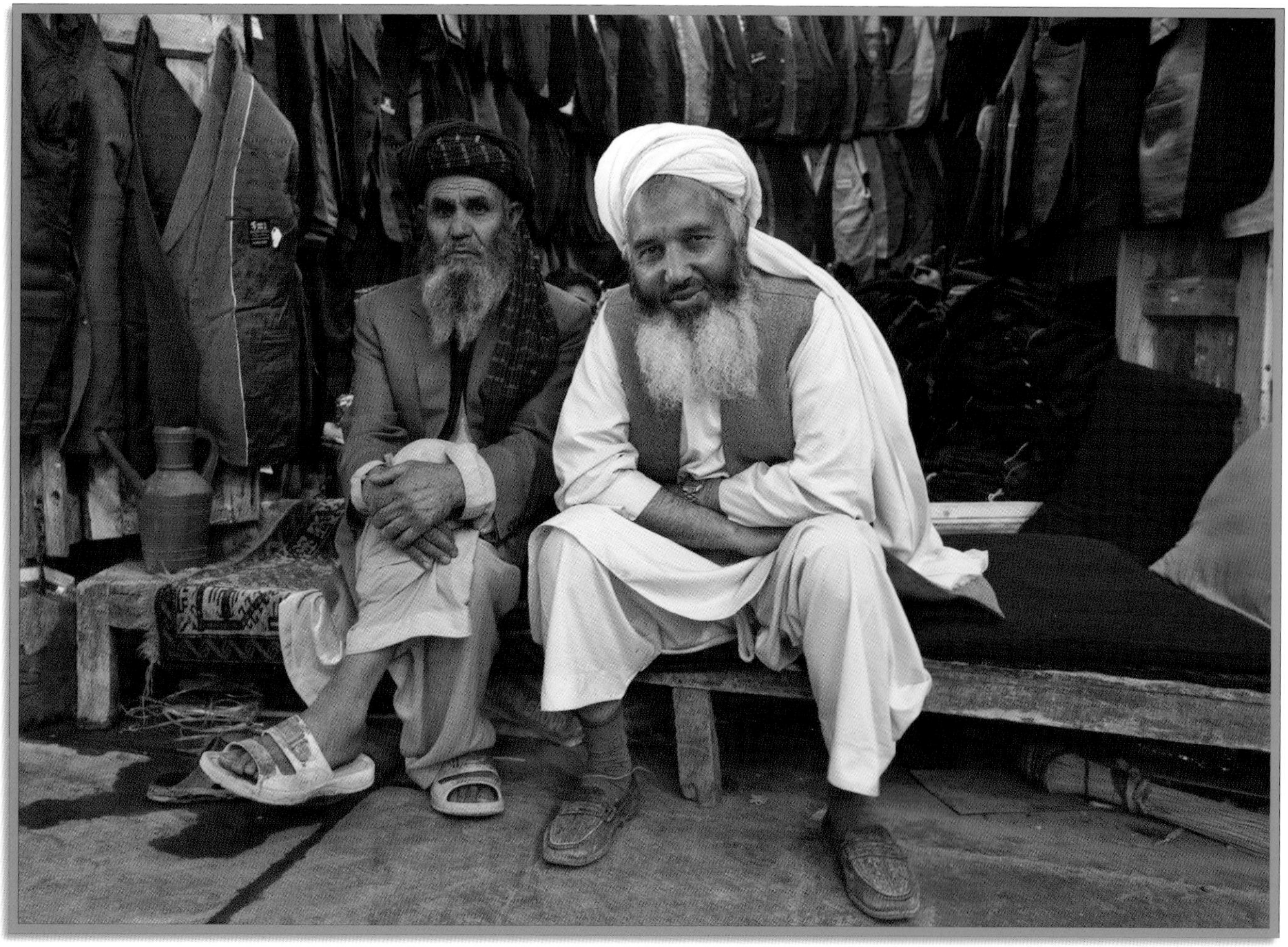

men

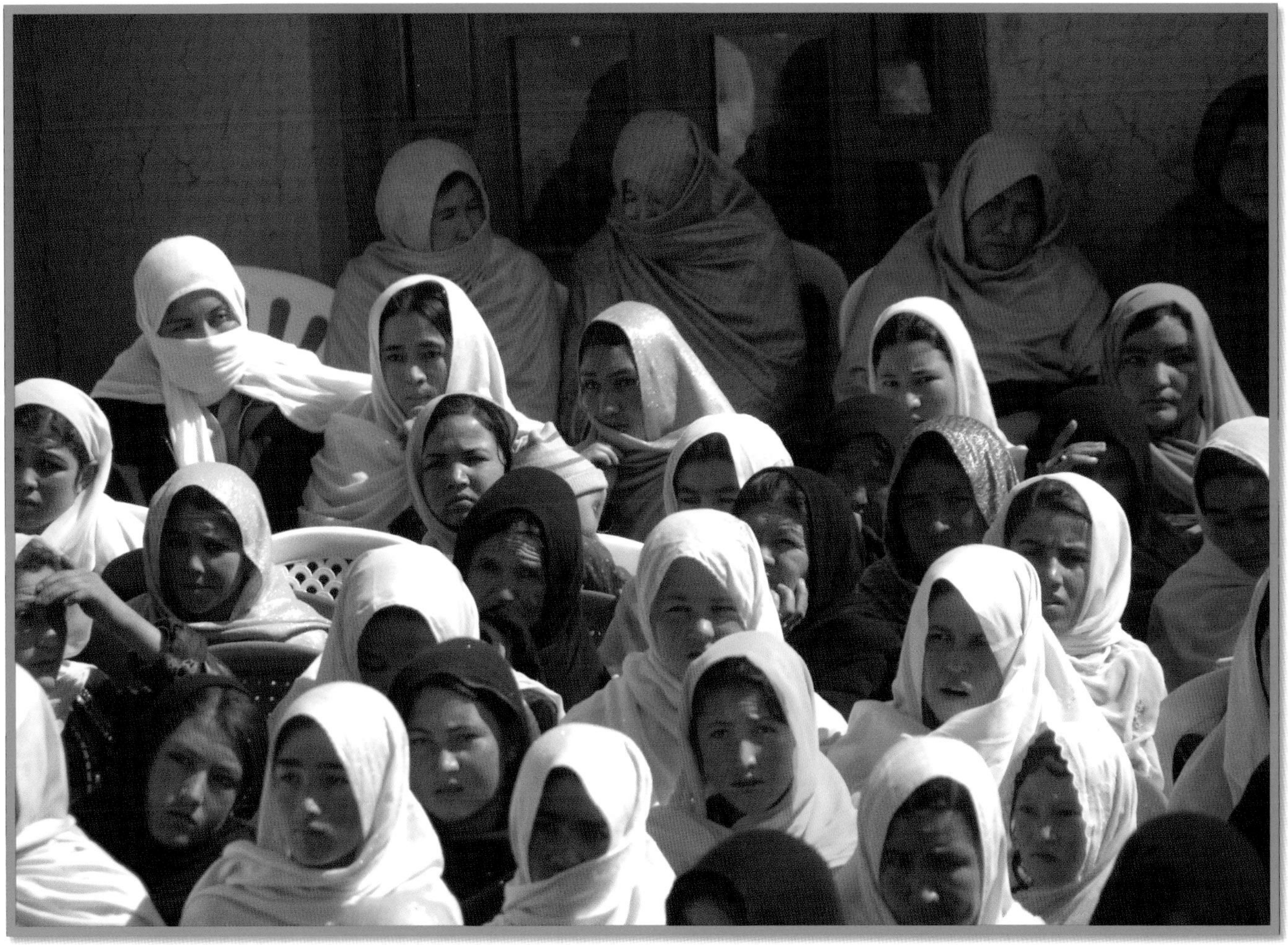

women

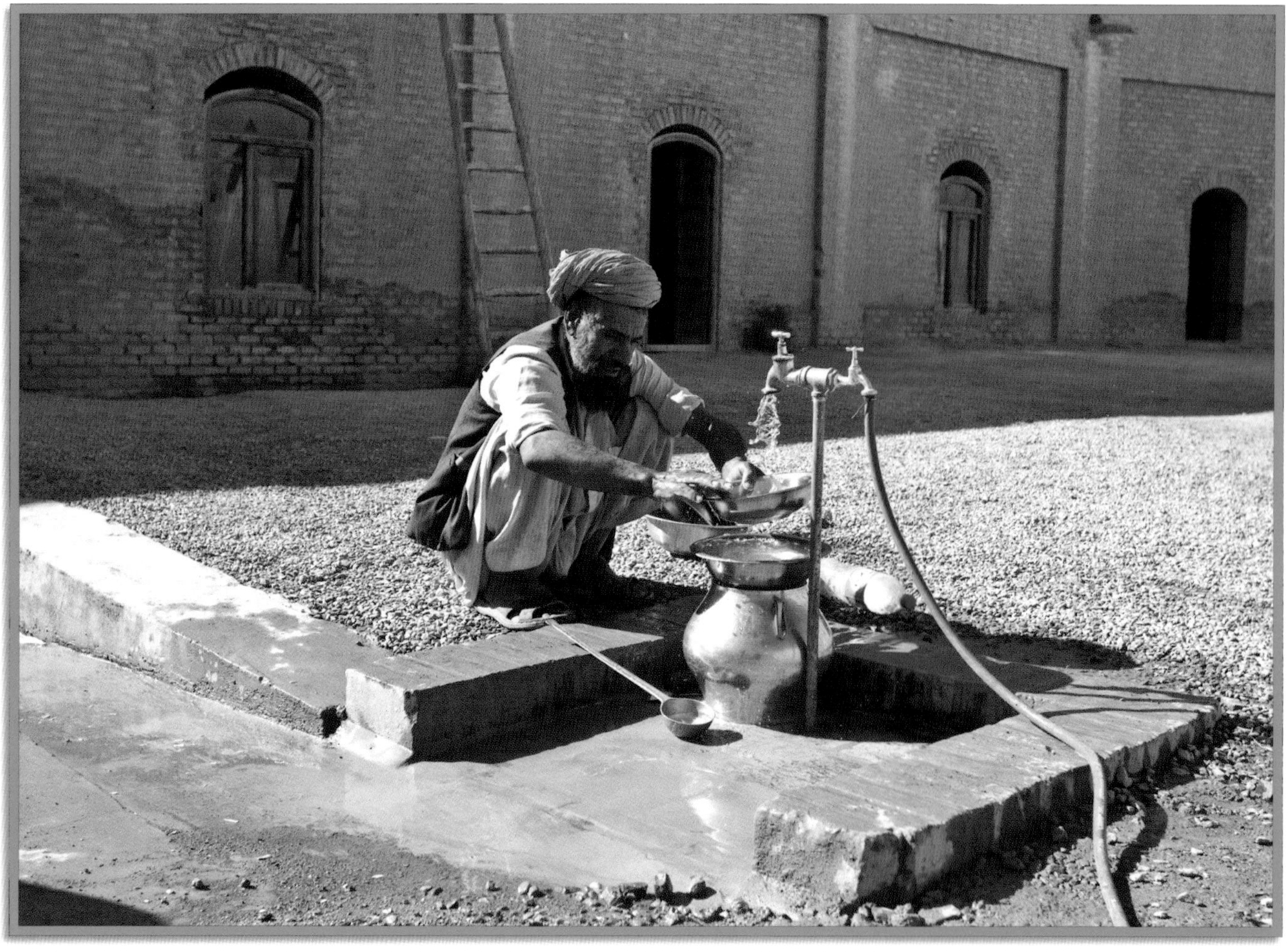

water

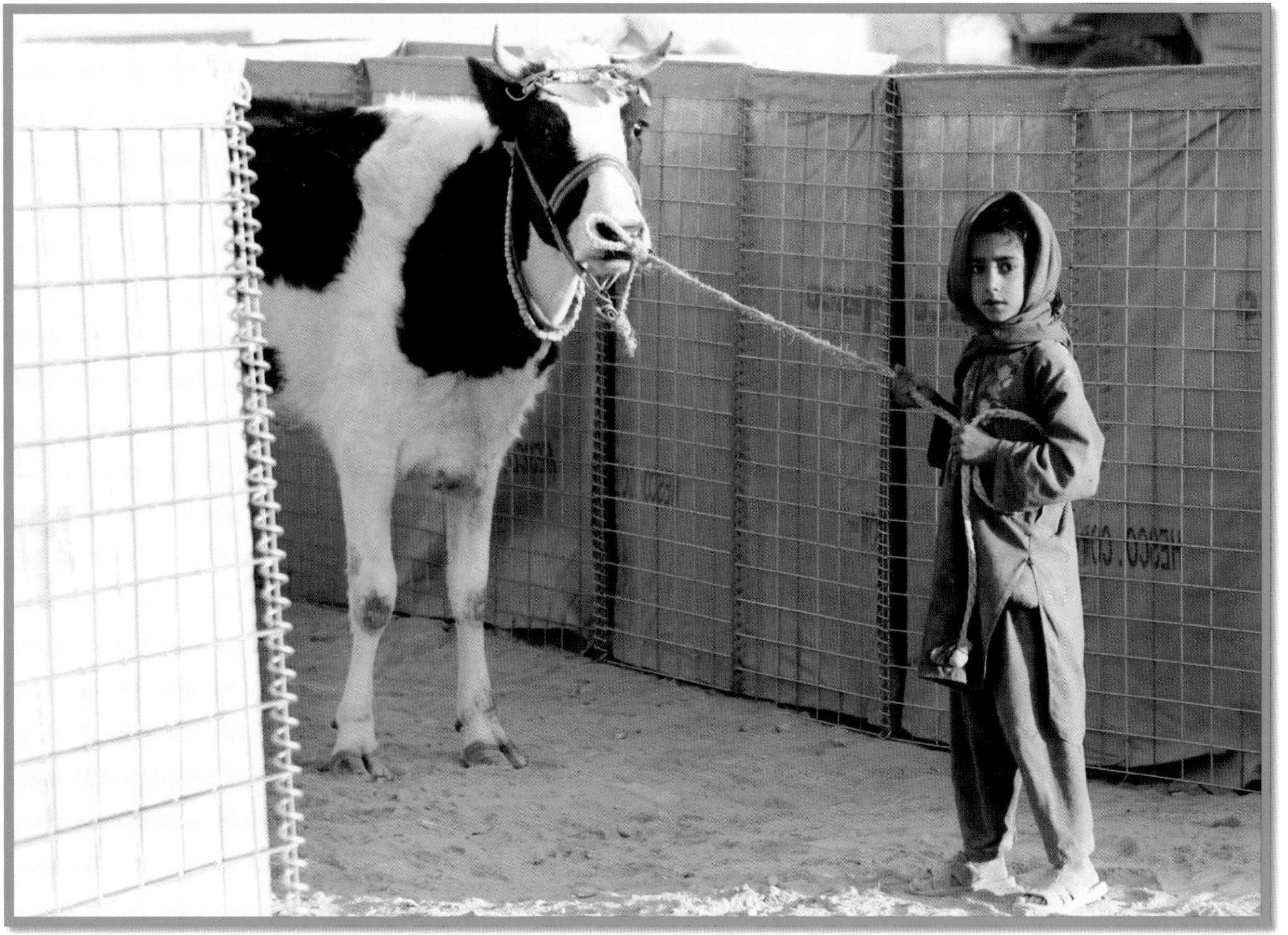

cow

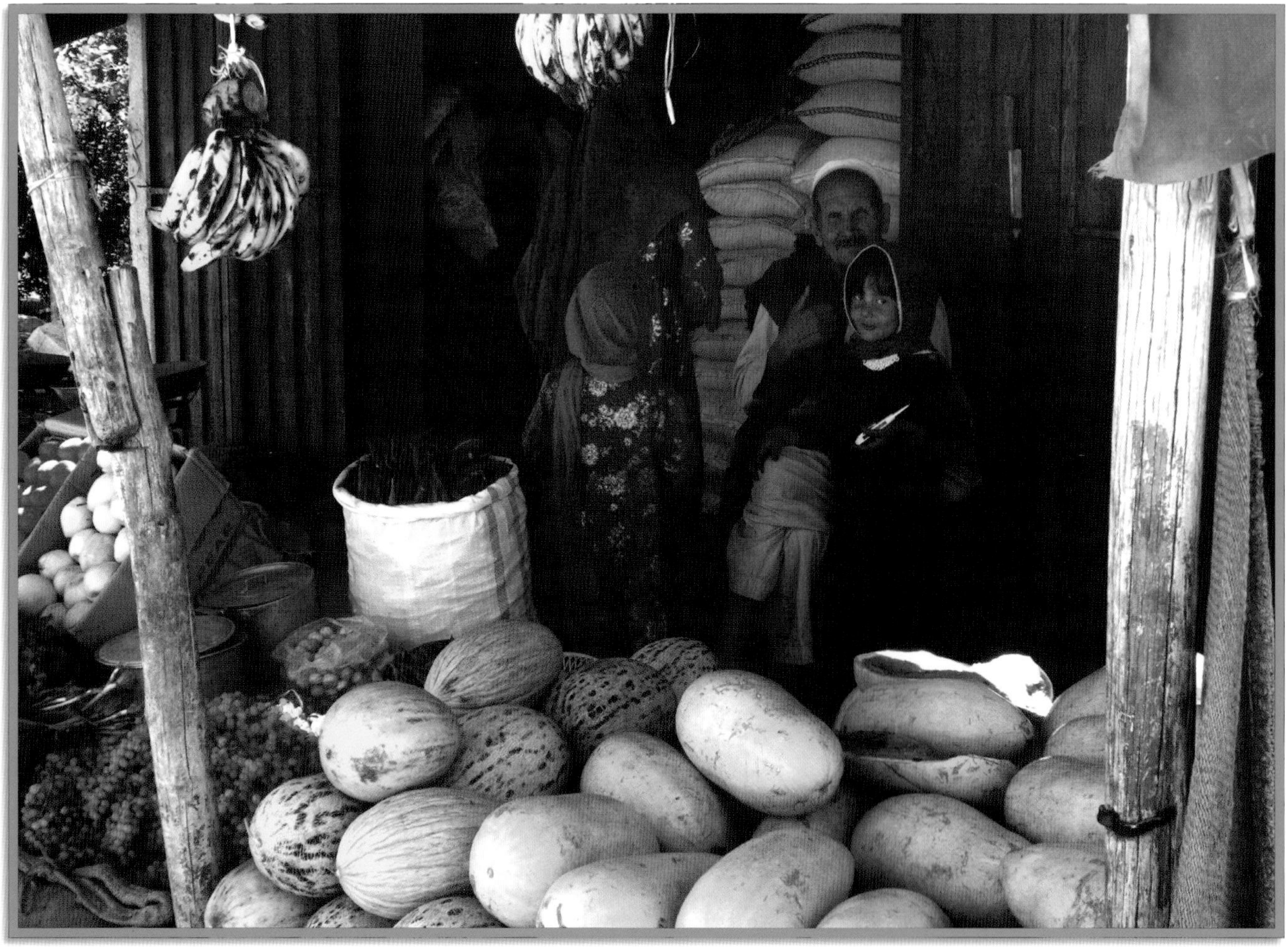

food

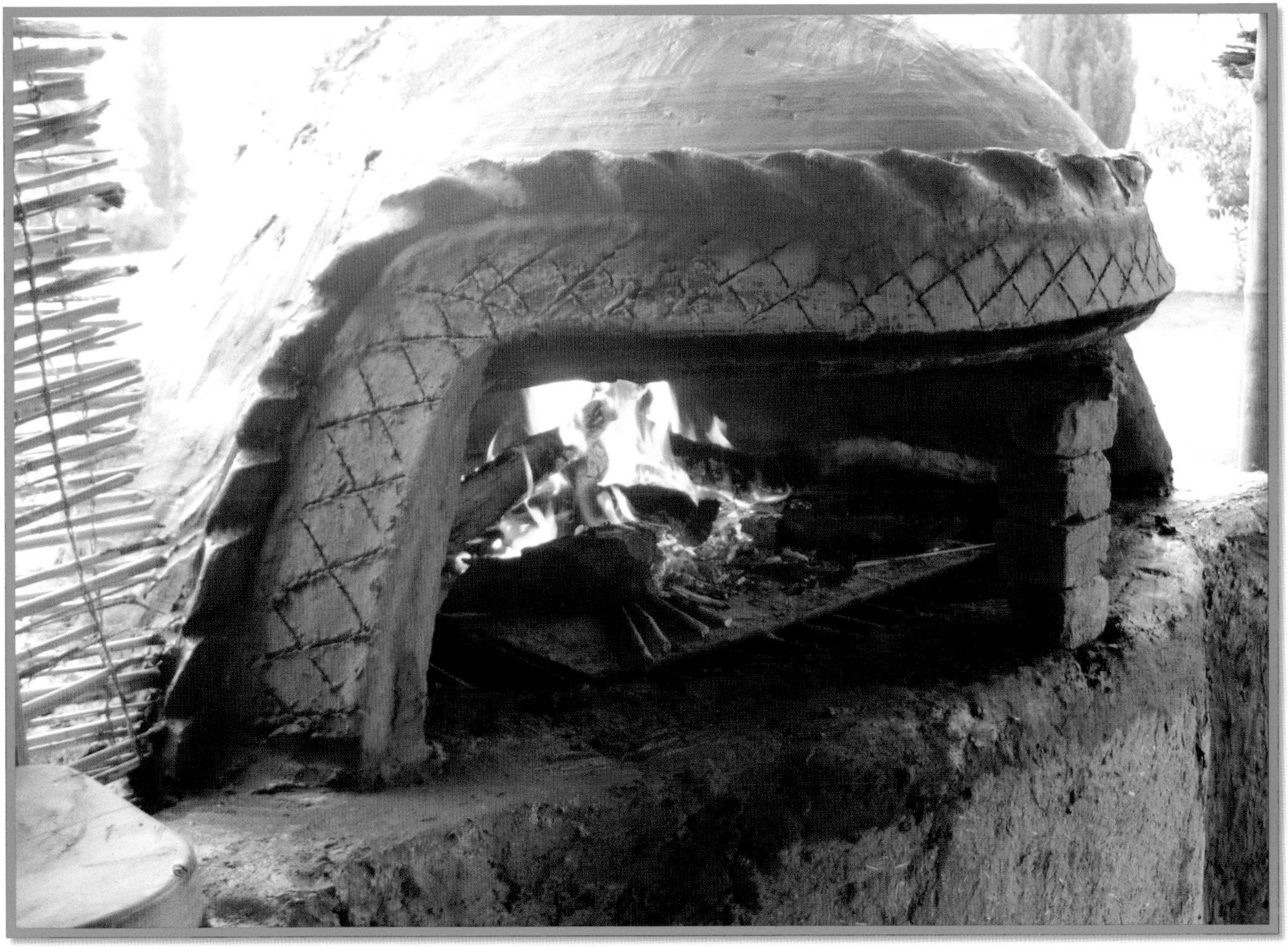

fire

Match the letter to the picture.

m

b

c

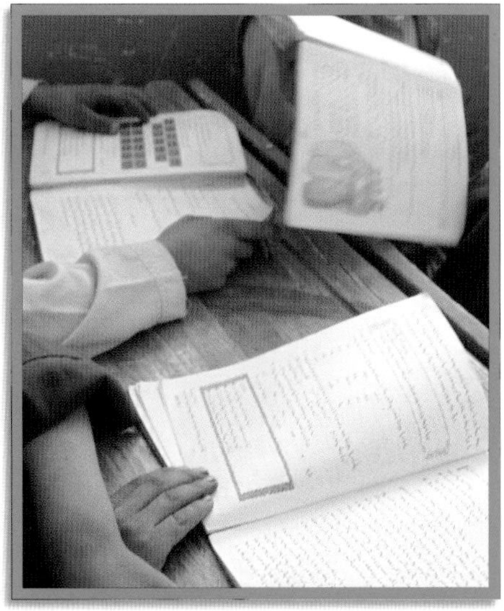

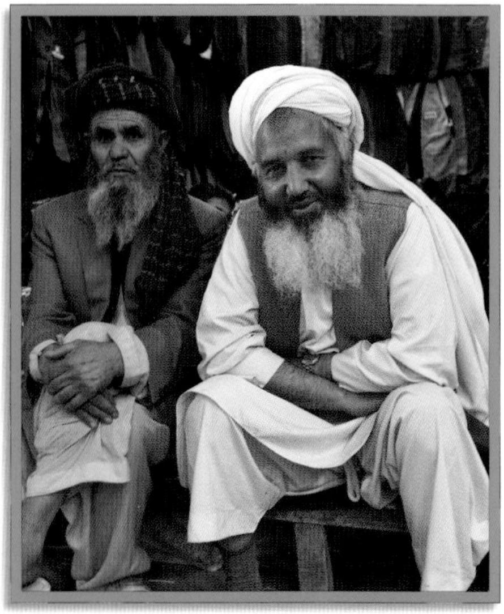

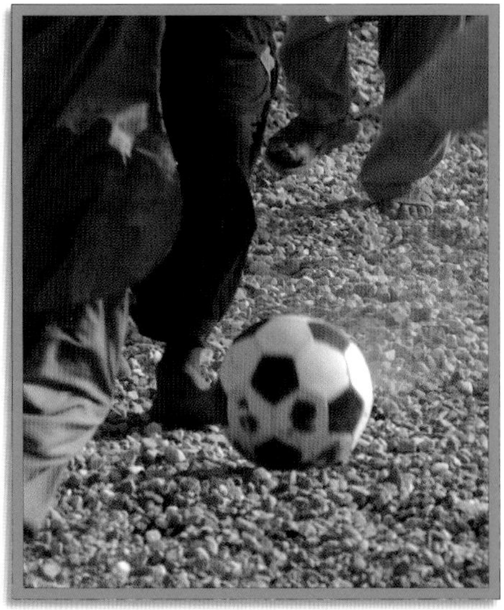

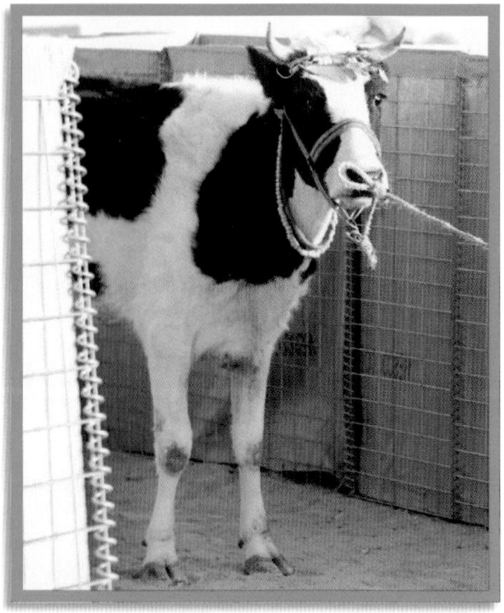